"Entrepreneurship: The Path to Success"

Description

"Entrepreneurship: The Path to Success" is an ebook that explores the journey of becoming a successful entrepreneur. The book covers a range of topics including developing a business idea, creating a business plan, securing funding, marketing and branding, and managing a team. The ebook provides practical tips and advice for navigating the challenges and opportunities of entrepreneurship, as well as insights from successful entrepreneurs. Whether you're just starting out or looking to take your business to the next level, "Entrepreneurship: The Path to Success" is an essential guide for anyone aspiring to succeed in the world of business.

Index

1. *Developing a clear business idea*
2. *Conducting market research*
3. *Identifying a target audience*
4. *Creating a business plan*
5. *Defining your brand*
6. *Networking with other entrepreneurs*
7. *Securing funding*
8. *Building a website*
9. *Establishing social media presence*
10. *Creating valuable content*
11. *Leveraging email marketing*
12. *Establishing a strong work ethic*
13. *Staying motivated and persistent*
14. *Continuously learning and improving*
15. *Building a strong team*
16. *Prioritizing customer satisfaction*
17. *Adapting to change and challenges*

18. *Managing finances effectively*
19. *Creating a positive company culture*
20. *Developing a marketing strategy*
21. *Monitoring industry trends*
22. *Embracing innovation*
23. *Seeking out mentorship and guidance*
24. *Investing in personal and professional growth*
25. *Establishing clear goals and objectives*
26. *Balancing work and personal life*
27. *Creating a strong personal brand*
28. *Collaborating with others*
29. *Embracing failure as a learning opportunity*
30. *Giving back to the community.*

Way 1
Developing a clear business idea

Developing a clear business idea is the crucial first step in the journey towards becoming a successful entrepreneur. Without a clear idea of what your business will be about, it will be difficult to create a plan, secure funding, and ultimately achieve success. In "Entrepreneurship: The Path to Success", this process is explored in-depth, offering guidance and advice to those looking to develop a clear and compelling business idea.

The first step in developing a business idea is to identify a problem that needs solving. Entrepreneurs are often successful because they have identified a gap in the market and developed a solution to meet the needs of their target audience. This could be a new product, service, or even a new way of delivering an existing solution. Identifying the problem is the first step towards creating a solution that people are willing to pay for.

Once you have identified a problem, the next step is to research the market. This involves identifying competitors, assessing demand, and understanding the size of the potential market. This is an important step in determining whether there is a viable opportunity to turn your idea into a successful business. If the market is saturated, or there is little demand for your product or service, it may be difficult to succeed.

When you have completed market research, you can begin to develop your unique selling proposition (USP). This is what will set your business apart from competitors and attract customers. Your USP could be the quality of your product, the level of customer service you provide, or the convenience of your delivery methods. Whatever it is, it should be something that resonates with your target audience and provides a compelling reason to choose your business over others.

The next step is to develop a business model. This involves determining how you will generate revenue, what costs you will incur, and how you will achieve profitability. There are many different business models to choose from, and the right one for your business will depend on a range of factors, including the nature of your product or service, the size of the market, and the level of competition.

Another important aspect of developing a clear business idea is identifying your target audience. This involves understanding the demographics, interests, and behaviours of your potential customers. Once you have a clear picture of your target audience, you can begin to tailor your marketing efforts and product development to meet their needs and preferences.

Once you have developed a clear idea of what your business will be, it is important to conduct a feasibility analysis. This involves assessing the viability of your business idea by looking at factors such as the level of demand for your product or service, the level of competition, and the costs involved in bringing your idea to market. If your analysis suggests that your idea is not viable, it may be necessary to go back to the drawing board and refine your idea or find a new opportunity.

Finally, it is important to develop a mission statement that articulates the purpose and values of your business. This statement should be concise and easy to understand, and should reflect the unique character of your business. A mission statement is important because it provides a clear direction for your business, and helps to create a sense of purpose and motivation among employees.

In summary, developing a clear business idea is the crucial first step towards becoming a successful entrepreneur. It involves identifying a problem that needs solving, conducting market research, developing a unique selling proposition, creating a business model, identifying your target audience, conducting a feasibility analysis, and developing a mission statement. By following these steps, you can develop a clear and compelling idea that has the potential to attract customers and generate revenue. With a clear business idea in place, you will be well on your way to achieving success as an entrepreneur.

Way 2
Conducting market research

Market research is a crucial step in starting and growing a successful business. It involves gathering and analyzing information about the market, customers, competition, and industry trends to make informed business decisions. In this article, we will explore the importance of market research and the steps involved in conducting effective market research.

Why Conduct Market Research?

Conducting market research is essential for several reasons. Firstly, it helps entrepreneurs identify business opportunities and gaps in the market. By understanding customer needs and preferences, entrepreneurs can develop products or services that meet those needs and differentiate themselves from their competitors. Market research also helps entrepreneurs make informed decisions about pricing, promotion, and distribution strategies.

Secondly, market research enables entrepreneurs to understand their target customers better. By gathering information on customer demographics, behavior, and preferences, entrepreneurs can tailor their marketing and advertising efforts to reach their target audience more effectively. This understanding can also help entrepreneurs identify potential barriers to entry and develop strategies to overcome them.

Finally, market research provides entrepreneurs with valuable insights into their competitors. By analyzing their competitors' strengths and weaknesses, entrepreneurs can develop strategies to differentiate themselves and gain a competitive advantage.

Steps Involved in Conducting Market Research

1. Define the Research Objectives

The first step in conducting market research is to define the research objectives. What are the questions you want to answer? What information do you need to make informed business decisions? Defining your research objectives will help you focus your research efforts and ensure that you gather the right data.

Identify the Target Market

The next step is to identify your target market. Who are your potential customers? What are their characteristics, needs, and preferences? Understanding your target market is essential for developing products or services that meet their needs and for tailoring your marketing efforts to reach them effectively.

1. Gather Data

Once you have defined your research objectives and identified your target market, the next step is to gather data. There are two types of data: primary data and secondary data. Primary data is data that you gather yourself, while secondary data is data that already exists, such as industry reports, government statistics, and competitor websites. Primary data can be collected through surveys, interviews, focus groups, or observation. Surveys are a popular method for gathering primary data and can be conducted online, by mail, or in person. Interviews and focus groups allow for more in-depth data collection and can provide valuable insights into customer behavior and preferences. Observation involves watching and recording customer behavior in real-time.

1. Analyze the Data

Once you have gathered your data, the next step is to analyze it. This involves organizing and interpreting the data to identify patterns and trends. The analysis should answer the research questions and provide insights into the target market, competition, and industry trends.

Draw Conclusions and Make Recommendations

The final step in conducting market research is to draw conclusions and make recommendations based on the data. This involves synthesizing the findings and translating them into actionable recommendations for the business. The recommendations should address the research objectives and provide guidance for making informed business decisions.

1. Conclusion

Conducting effective market research is essential for entrepreneurs who want to start and grow a successful business. It provides valuable insights into the target market, competition, and industry trends, and helps entrepreneurs make informed business decisions. By following the steps outlined in this article, entrepreneurs can gather and analyze the data they need to develop products or services that meet customer needs, tailor their marketing efforts to reach their target audience, and gain a competitive advantage in the marketplace.

Way 3
Identifying a target audience

Entrepreneurship has become a popular topic in recent years as more people seek to become their own boss and create a successful business. However, the path to success is not always easy, and not everyone is cut out for the challenges that come with starting a business. To identify a target audience for a discussion on entrepreneurship, it is important to understand who might benefit from this information and what their goals and challenges are.

Firstly, individuals who are interested in entrepreneurship may have a variety of motivations for wanting to start their own business. Some may be seeking financial independence or the ability to control their own schedule, while others may have a passion for a particular product or service that they want to bring to market. These individuals may be at different stages of their entrepreneurial journey, ranging from those who are just starting to explore the idea to those who have already launched a business and are seeking advice on how to grow and scale.

Another potential target audience for a discussion on entrepreneurship is young people who are just starting their careers. Many young people today are facing a tough job market and may be interested in exploring alternative paths to success. Starting a business can be a viable option for those who are willing to take on the risk and hard work that comes with entrepreneurship. However, it is important to note that young people may have unique challenges that need to be addressed, such as lack of experience or access to capital.

In addition to young people, individuals who are already in the workforce may also be interested in entrepreneurship. This group may include those who are dissatisfied with their current job or seeking a career change, as well as those who are looking to supplement their income with a side business. These individuals may have more experience and resources than younger entrepreneurs, but they may also have more responsibilities and less flexibility in their schedules.

Entrepreneurship can also be a viable option for individuals who are nearing retirement age or who have already retired. Many people in this group may be looking for ways to stay active and engaged in their later years, and starting a business can provide a sense of purpose and fulfillment.

However, it is important to note that older entrepreneurs may face unique challenges, such as age discrimination and difficulty accessing capital.

Another potential target audience for a discussion on entrepreneurship is individuals who are part of marginalized communities. Starting a business can be an effective way for these individuals to create economic opportunities for themselves and their communities. However, it is important to acknowledge that these individuals may face additional barriers, such as lack of access to resources and discrimination. It is important to provide targeted support and resources for these entrepreneurs to ensure that they have an equal opportunity to succeed.

Finally, individuals who are interested in social entrepreneurship may be another target audience for a discussion on entrepreneurship. Social entrepreneurship involves starting a business with the goal of creating positive social or environmental impact, in addition to generating profit. This type of entrepreneurship may appeal to individuals who are passionate about a particular cause or issue and want to make a difference in the world. However, it is important to note that social entrepreneurship may have unique challenges and require different skills and resources than traditional entrepreneurship.

In conclusion, there are many potential target audiences for a discussion on entrepreneurship, each with their own goals, challenges, and unique circumstances. By understanding the needs and motivations of these different groups, we can provide more targeted and effective support for aspiring entrepreneurs and increase their chances of success.

WAy 4
Creating a business plan

Creating a business plan is a crucial step in the entrepreneurial journey. A business plan serves as a roadmap for the business, outlining its goals, strategies, and operations. It also provides a way for the entrepreneur to communicate their vision to potential investors, partners, and customers. In this summary, we will discuss the key elements of a business plan.

The first section of a business plan is the executive summary. This section provides an overview of the business, including its mission statement, products or services, target market, and competitive advantage. It should be concise and compelling, grabbing the reader's attention and giving them a sense of what the business is all about.

The next section is the company description, which provides more detailed information about the business. This may include information about the company's history, ownership structure, legal status, and location. It may also include a description of the team, including the founders and key employees, and their relevant experience and qualifications.

The market analysis section is where the entrepreneur provides an in-depth analysis of the industry and market in which their business operates. This may include information about the size of the market, key trends and challenges, and the target customer demographics. It is important to include a competitive analysis in this section, identifying key competitors and their strengths and weaknesses.

The next section is the product or service description, which provides detailed information about the products or services the business will offer. This may include information about the product features, pricing, and distribution channels. It is important to clearly define the unique value proposition of the product or service and how it will meet the needs of the target customer.

The marketing and sales section outlines the strategies the business will use to reach and acquire customers. This may include information about advertising and promotion, pricing strategies, and sales channels. It is important to include a detailed sales forecast in this section, outlining the expected revenue and growth projections for the business.

The operations and management section outlines the day-to-day operations of the business, including information about production, logistics, and personnel. This section may also include information about the legal and regulatory environment in which the business operates, as well as any intellectual property or patents that the business holds.

The financial projections section is where the entrepreneur provides detailed financial information about the business. This may include projected income statements, balance sheets, and cash flow statements. It is important to include realistic and conservative assumptions in these projections, as well as a detailed analysis of the costs and revenues associated with each business activity.

The final section of the business plan is the appendix, which includes any additional information that may be relevant to the business. This may include resumes of key personnel, market research reports, and legal documents.

In conclusion, creating a business plan is a critical step in the entrepreneurial journey. It provides a roadmap for the business and communicates the entrepreneur's vision to potential investors, partners, and customers. A good business plan includes a clear and compelling executive summary, a thorough market analysis, a detailed product or service description, a comprehensive marketing and sales strategy, a thorough operations and management plan, realistic financial projections, and relevant supporting information in the appendix. By creating a well-crafted business plan, entrepreneurs can increase their chances of success and make their vision a reality.

Way 5
Defining your brand

Defining your brand is a crucial step towards building a successful entrepreneurial venture. Your brand is essentially the identity of your business, encompassing everything from your mission statement and values to your logo and messaging. It's the foundation upon which your business is built and how your customers will come to know and trust your products or services.

To define your brand, start by clearly articulating your mission statement. This should be a succinct statement that encapsulates the purpose and values of your business. It should be easy to understand and communicate to your customers, and act as a guiding principle for your decision making.

Next, consider your target audience. Who are the people that your product or service is aimed at? What are their needs and wants? Understanding your target audience is key to creating a brand that resonates with them and effectively communicates the value of your offering.

Once you have a clear understanding of your mission and target audience, you can begin to craft your brand messaging. This includes developing a unique value proposition that sets you apart from competitors, as well as a brand voice that reflects your company's personality and tone.

A strong visual identity is also essential to defining your brand. This includes creating a logo, selecting a colour palette, and developing visual elements that reflect your brand's personality and values. Your visual identity should be consistent across all platforms, including your website, social media, and any other marketing materials.

It's also important to consider the overall user experience of your brand. This includes everything from the usability of your website to the packaging of your products. Providing a seamless and enjoyable user experience is key to building customer loyalty and creating a strong brand identity.

Finally, it's important to ensure that your brand is consistent across all touchpoints. This means ensuring that your messaging and visual identity are consistent across all marketing channels, including your website, social media, and any other communication channels.

In summary, defining your brand is a critical component of building a successful entrepreneurial venture. This involves creating a clear mission statement, understanding your target audience, developing strong brand messaging and a unique value proposition, creating a consistent visual identity, and providing a seamless user experience. By focusing on these key elements, you can create a brand that resonates with your customers and builds trust and loyalty over time

Way 6
Networking with other entrepreneurs

Networking with other entrepreneurs is an essential aspect of building a successful business. It allows entrepreneurs to build relationships with like-minded individuals, share knowledge and resources, and gain access to new opportunities. Here are some tips for effective networking:

1. Attend networking events: There are many networking events specifically designed for entrepreneurs. Attending these events can provide valuable opportunities to meet other entrepreneurs, exchange ideas, and learn from others. Look for events in your local area, and consider attending events in other cities or countries to expand your network.
1. Join online communities: Online communities such as social media groups, forums, and industry-specific networks can provide an easy way to connect with other entrepreneurs. Join relevant groups and participate in discussions to build relationships with others in your field.
1. Be genuine and authentic: Networking is all about building relationships, and the best relationships are built on trust and authenticity. Be yourself and be honest about your goals and challenges. Listen to others and offer genuine support and encouragement.
1. Focus on giving, not just taking: Successful networking is not just about what you can get from others, but also about what you can give. Look for opportunities to help others and offer

*your expertise and resources. This can help
you build a positive reputation and create
valuable relationships.*

1. *Follow up and stay in touch: After meeting
   someone at a networking event, be sure to
   follow up and stay in touch. This could mean
   sending an email or a LinkedIn message, or
   scheduling a follow-up call or meeting. Staying
   in touch can help build a long-term relationship
   that could lead to future opportunities.*

1. *Collaborate with other entrepreneurs:
   Collaborating with other entrepreneurs can
   provide valuable opportunities to share
   resources, pool knowledge and expertise, and
   tackle bigger projects. Look for opportunities to
   work on joint ventures, partnerships, or co-
   creation initiatives with other entrepreneurs.*

1. *Join a mentorship program: Mentorship
   programs can provide valuable opportunities to
   learn from experienced entrepreneurs and gain
   access to their networks. Look for mentorship
   programs in your field, and consider joining as
   either a mentor or a mentee.*

1. *Attend industry conferences: Attending
   industry conferences can provide opportunities
   to meet other entrepreneurs and industry
   leaders, learn about new trends and
   developments, and gain exposure for your
   business. Look for conferences in your field,
   and consider speaking or presenting to
   showcase your expertise.*

*In summary, networking with other entrepreneurs is an
essential part of building a successful business. It involves
attending networking events, joining online communities,
being genuine and authentic, focusing on giving, following
up and staying in touch, collaborating with others, joining a
mentorship program, and attending industry conferences. By
building strong relationships with other entrepreneurs, you
can gain valuable insights and resources, expand your*

network, and create new opportunities for growth and success

Way 7
Securing funding

Securing funding is a crucial step for entrepreneurs looking to turn their business ideas into reality. Here are some key points to consider when seeking funding for your venture:

1. *Understand your business needs: Before you start approaching investors or lenders, it's important to have a clear understanding of your funding requirements. This includes determining how much money you need, how you plan to use the funds, and what type of funding is most suitable for your business.*
1. *Explore funding options: There are several ways to secure funding, including bank loans, angel investors, venture capital firms, crowdfunding, and government grants. Each option has its own pros and cons, and the right choice will depend on your business's specific needs and goals.*
1. *Develop a business plan: A solid business plan is a critical tool for securing funding. It should include a detailed description of your business, market analysis, financial projections, and an overview of your funding needs. Your plan should be clear, concise, and compelling.*
1. *Build a strong network: Building relationships with potential investors or lenders is an important part of securing funding. Attend industry events, join networking groups, and seek out mentorship opportunities to expand your network.*
1. *Prepare a pitch: When meeting with potential investors, be prepared to give a concise and compelling pitch that outlines your business*

idea, its potential for success, and your funding needs. Make sure to highlight your unique selling proposition and explain how your business will generate revenue.

1. Be transparent: Investors will want to see a clear understanding of your business's risks and challenges. Be honest and transparent about the potential risks, and be prepared to offer solutions to mitigate them.
1. Demonstrate traction: Investors are often more willing to fund businesses that have already demonstrated traction. This includes evidence of a strong customer base, revenue growth, or promising partnerships.
1. Negotiate terms: Once you have secured interest from investors, it's important to negotiate favourable terms. This includes understanding the terms of the investment, such as the amount of equity you will be giving up or the repayment terms of a loan.
1. Seek professional advice: Seeking professional advice from lawyers, accountants, and financial advisors can help you navigate the complexities of securing funding. These experts can provide valuable guidance and help ensure you are making informed decisions.

In conclusion, securing funding is an essential step in the entrepreneurial journey. By understanding your business needs, exploring funding options, developing a solid business plan, building a strong network, preparing a compelling pitch, being transparent, demonstrating traction, negotiating favourable terms, and seeking professional advice, you can increase your chances of securing the funding you need to turn your business idea into a reality

Way 8

Building a website

In today's digital age, having a website is essential for any business, including entrepreneurs looking to build a successful venture. Here are some key points to consider when building a website:

1. Define your website's purpose: Before you start building your website, it's important to define its purpose. Are you using it to sell products or services, generate leads, or build brand awareness? Knowing your website's purpose will help guide its design and content.

1. Choose a domain name: Your domain name is your website's address, so it's important to choose a name that is memorable and easy to spell. Consider using your business name or a keyword related to your industry.

1. Select a hosting provider: Your website needs to be hosted on a server to be accessible on the internet. There are many hosting providers to choose from, and the right choice will depend on your website's needs and budget.

1. Choose a website builder: There are several website builders available that make it easy for entrepreneurs to build a website without needing technical skills. These builders typically offer a range of templates and design options.

1. Design your website: Your website's design should be visually appealing and easy to navigate. It should also be consistent with your brand's colours and messaging. Be sure to include clear calls-to-action, such as "Contact Us" or "Buy Now" buttons.

1. Create engaging content: Your website's content should be engaging, informative, and relevant to your target audience. This includes writing clear and compelling copy, as well as

including images and videos that help tell your brand's story.
1. Optimise for search engines: Search engine optimisation (SEO) is the practice of improving your website's visibility on search engine results pages. This involves using relevant keywords in your website's content, as well as ensuring your website is mobile-friendly and has fast load times.
1. Integrate social media: Social media is an important tool for building brand awareness and driving traffic to your website. Make sure to include social media buttons on your website, as well as shareable content that can be easily posted to social media.
1. Test and launch: Before launching your website, be sure to test it thoroughly to ensure it is functioning properly and free of errors. This includes testing all links and forms, as well as ensuring your website looks good on a range of devices and web browsers.
1. Monitor and update: Once your website is live, it's important to monitor its performance and make updates as necessary. This includes tracking website traffic, making changes to your content or design, and ensuring your website is secure and up-to-date.

In conclusion, building a website is an important step for any entrepreneur looking to build a successful business. By defining your website's purpose, choosing a domain name, selecting a hosting provider, choosing a website builder, designing your website, creating engaging content, optimising for search engines, integrating social media, testing and launching, and monitoring and updating, you can build a website that effectively communicates your brand's message and helps drive business growth.

Way 9

Establishing social media presence

In today's digital age, having a strong social media presence is essential for any business, including entrepreneurs looking to build a successful venture. Here are some key points to consider when establishing a social media presence:

1. Define your social media strategy: Before you start establishing a social media presence, it's important to define your strategy. What are your social media goals? Who is your target audience? Which social media platforms are best suited for your business? These are all important questions to consider when defining your social media strategy.
1. Choose the right platforms: There are many social media platforms to choose from, including Facebook, Instagram, Twitter, LinkedIn, and more. Each platform has its own strengths and weaknesses, and it's important to choose the platforms that are most relevant to your target audience.
1. Create a content plan: A strong social media presence requires a consistent stream of engaging content. It's important to create a content plan that includes a mix of text, images, and videos that align with your brand's messaging and resonate with your target audience.
1. Engage with your audience: Social media is a two-way conversation. It's important to engage with your audience by responding to comments and messages, sharing user-generated content, and running social media contests and promotions.

1. *Leverage social media advertising: Social media advertising can be a cost-effective way to reach a larger audience and drive business growth. Platforms like Facebook and Instagram offer a range of targeting options to help you reach your ideal customer.*
1. *Monitor your social media metrics: It's important to monitor your social media metrics to understand how your content is performing and make adjustments as necessary. This includes tracking metrics like reach, engagement, and conversions.*
1. *Keep up-to-date with social media trends: Social media is constantly evolving, and it's important to stay up-to-date with the latest trends and best practices. This includes attending industry conferences, reading social media blogs, and networking with other social media professionals.*

In conclusion, establishing a strong social media presence is an important step for any entrepreneur looking to build a successful business. By defining your social media strategy, choosing the right platforms, creating a content plan, engaging with your audience, leveraging social media advertising, monitoring your social media metrics, and keeping up-to-date with social media trends, you can build a social media presence that effectively communicates your brand's message and helps drive business growth.

Way 10
Creating valuable content

Creating valuable content is an essential part of building a successful business, as it helps to establish credibility, build brand awareness, and attract and retain customers. Here are some key points to consider when creating valuable content:

1. *Define your target audience: Before you start creating content, it's important to define your target audience. Who are you trying to reach with your content? What are their interests and pain points? This information will help guide the topics and tone of your content.*
1. *Choose the right format: There are many different types of content, including blog posts, videos, infographics, podcasts, and more. It's important to choose the format that best aligns with your brand's messaging and resonates with your target audience.*
1. *Develop a content calendar: A strong content strategy requires a consistent stream of high-quality content. It's important to develop a content calendar that includes a mix of evergreen and timely topics, and aligns with your overall marketing goals.*
1. *Write compelling headlines: Your content's headline is often the first thing that readers see, so it's important to make it compelling and attention-grabbing. A good headline should be clear, concise, and give readers a reason to read on.*
1. *Focus on quality over quantity: While it's important to have a consistent stream of content, it's more important to focus on quality over quantity. Your content should be well-researched, informative, and valuable to your target audience.*
1. *Use visual aids: Visual aids like images, videos, and infographics can help make your content more engaging and shareable. They can also help to break up long blocks of text and make your content more scannable.*
1. *Optimise for search engines: Search engine optimisation (SEO) is the practice of improving your content's visibility on search engine results pages. This involves using relevant*

keywords in your content, as well as ensuring your content is mobile-friendly and has fast load times.

1. *Promote your content:* Once you've created valuable content, it's important to promote it to ensure it reaches your target audience. This can include sharing your content on social media, running email marketing campaigns, and collaborating with other brands and influencers.

1. *Monitor your content's performance:* It's important to monitor your content's performance to understand what is resonating with your target audience and make adjustments as necessary. This includes tracking metrics like page views, time on page, and social shares.

1. *Continuously iterate and improve:* Building a strong content strategy is an ongoing process. It's important to continuously iterate and improve your content based on feedback from your target audience and changes in the industry.

In conclusion, creating valuable content is an important part of building a successful business. By defining your target audience, choosing the right format, developing a content calendar, writing compelling headlines, focusing on quality over quantity, using visual aids, optimising for search engines, promoting your content, monitoring your content's performance, and continuously iterating and improving, you can create a content strategy that effectively communicates your brand's message and helps drive business growth.

Way 11
Leveraging email marketing

Email marketing is a powerful tool for entrepreneurs to engage with customers, build brand loyalty, and drive sales.

Here are some key points to consider when leveraging email marketing:

1. *Build a high-quality email list: A high-quality email list is the foundation of any successful email marketing campaign. It's important to focus on building a list of engaged, opt-in subscribers who are interested in your brand and products.*
1. *Choose the right email service provider: An email service provider (ESP) is a platform that allows you to send and manage email campaigns. It's important to choose an ESP that offers the features and integrations you need, as well as one that is user-friendly and reliable.*
1. *Personalise your emails: Personalisation is a key component of effective email marketing. By using subscriber data to personalise emails, you can create a more engaging and relevant experience for your subscribers, which can help drive higher open and click-through rates.*
1. *Segment your email list: Segmentation involves dividing your email list into smaller groups based on factors like demographics, past purchase behaviour, and email engagement. This allows you to tailor your emails to specific groups, which can help improve engagement and conversion rates.*
1. *Use automation: Email automation allows you to set up triggered emails that are sent automatically based on subscriber actions. For example, you can send a welcome email when someone joins your list or a cart abandonment email when someone leaves items in their cart without completing a purchase.*
1. *Focus on delivering value: Your email content should focus on delivering value to your subscribers, whether that's through informative*

content, exclusive discounts, or early access to new products. By providing value, you can build trust and loyalty with your subscribers, which can lead to increased sales over time.

1. *Use compelling subject lines: Your subject line is the first thing that subscribers see, so it's important to make it compelling and attention-grabbing. A good subject line should be clear, concise, and give subscribers a reason to open your email.*

1. *Include a clear call to action: Every email you send should have a clear call to action (CTA), whether that's to make a purchase, sign up for a free trial, or read a blog post. Your CTA should be prominent and easy to find within your email.*

1. *Test and optimise your campaigns: Email marketing is an ongoing process of testing and optimising. It's important to track metrics like open and click-through rates, as well as conversion rates, and make adjustments to your campaigns as needed to improve performance.*

1. *Comply with email marketing regulations: Email marketing is subject to regulations like GDPR and CAN-SPAM. It's important to ensure that you are complying with these regulations to avoid penalties and maintain the trust of your subscribers.*

In conclusion, email marketing is a powerful tool for entrepreneurs looking to engage with customers and drive sales. By building a high-quality email list, choosing the right ESP, personalising your emails, segmenting your email list, using automation, focusing on delivering value, using compelling subject lines, including a clear call to action, testing and optimising your campaigns, and complying with email marketing regulations, you can create effective email campaigns that help you achieve your business goals.

Way 12
Establishing a strong work ethic

Establishing a strong work ethic is a key component of success for any entrepreneur. Here are some key points to consider when building a strong work ethic:

1. *Set clear goals: Establishing clear, achievable goals is essential for developing a strong work ethic. It's important to set goals that are specific, measurable, and time-bound, and to track your progress towards these goals regularly.*
1. *Prioritise your time: Time management is a crucial aspect of developing a strong work ethic. It's important to prioritise your time and focus on the most important tasks first, while also leaving time for rest and relaxation.*
1. *Be self-motivated: Developing a strong work ethic also requires self-motivation. It's important to stay focused and disciplined, even when faced with challenges or setbacks.*
1. *Embrace challenges: Challenges and failures are a natural part of the entrepreneurial journey. It's important to embrace these challenges and learn from them, rather than being discouraged by them.*
1. *Cultivate resilience: Building a strong work ethic also requires resilience. This means being able to bounce back from setbacks and continue working towards your goals, even in the face of adversity.*
1. *Practice self-care: Taking care of yourself is a critical aspect of developing a strong work ethic. This means getting enough sleep, eating a healthy diet, and engaging in regular*

exercise, as well as taking time to pursue hobbies and other activities outside of work.

1. Surround yourself with like-minded individuals: Surrounding yourself with supportive, like-minded individuals can help you stay motivated and focused on your goals. Consider joining networking groups or finding a mentor who can provide guidance and support.
1. Continuously learn and grow: Developing a strong work ethic requires a commitment to continuous learning and growth. This means seeking out new information, staying up-to-date on industry trends, and pursuing professional development opportunities.
1. Be accountable: Taking responsibility for your actions is an important part of developing a strong work ethic. This means holding yourself accountable for your successes and failures, and learning from both.
1. Celebrate successes: Finally, celebrating your successes is an important part of building a strong work ethic. Take time to acknowledge and celebrate your achievements, no matter how small, and use these successes as motivation to continue working towards your goals.

In conclusion, developing a strong work ethic is critical for success as an entrepreneur. By setting clear goals, prioritising your time, being self-motivated, embracing challenges, cultivating resilience, practicing self-care, surrounding yourself with like-minded individuals, continuously learning and growing, being accountable, and celebrating successes, you can build a strong work ethic that will help you achieve your business goals.

Way13

Staying motivated and persistent

Staying motivated and persistent is essential for success as an entrepreneur. Here are some key points to consider when trying to maintain motivation and persistence:

1. *Define your "why": To stay motivated and persistent, it's important to understand why you're pursuing your entrepreneurial venture in the first place. Defining your "why" can help you stay focused and motivated, even when faced with challenges or setbacks.*
1. *Set achievable goals: Setting achievable goals is crucial for maintaining motivation and persistence. These goals should be specific, measurable, and time-bound, and should be broken down into smaller, manageable steps.*
1. *Celebrate small victories: Celebrating small victories along the way can help you stay motivated and persistent. By acknowledging and celebrating progress, you can maintain a sense of momentum and feel more positive about your overall progress.*
1. *Build a support system: Building a support system of like-minded individuals can help you stay motivated and persistent. This can include friends, family members, mentors, and other entrepreneurs who can provide encouragement and support when you need it.*
1. *Practice self-care: Taking care of yourself is essential for maintaining motivation and persistence. This means getting enough sleep, eating a healthy diet, and engaging in regular exercise, as well as taking time to pursue hobbies and other activities outside of work.*
1. *Stay organized: Staying organized can help you stay focused and motivated. This means*

having a clear plan for your daily tasks and priorities, as well as keeping your workspace tidy and clutter-free.

1. *Embrace challenges: Challenges are an inevitable part of the entrepreneurial journey. Embracing these challenges and viewing them as opportunities to learn and grow can help you stay motivated and persistent, even in the face of setbacks.*
1. *Learn from failures: Failure is a natural part of entrepreneurship. By viewing failures as opportunities to learn and grow, you can maintain a sense of motivation and persistence even when faced with setbacks.*
1. *Visualize success: Visualizing success can help you stay motivated and persistent. This means picturing what your business will look like when it's successful, and using this mental image as motivation to keep working towards your goals.*
1. *Practice gratitude: Finally, practicing gratitude can help you stay motivated and persistent. By focusing on the positive aspects of your entrepreneurial journey and expressing gratitude for the opportunities you've been given, you can maintain a positive mindset and stay motivated to continue pursuing your goals.*

In conclusion, staying motivated and persistent is essential for success as an entrepreneur. By defining your "why," setting achievable goals, celebrating small victories, building a support system, practicing self-care, staying organized, embracing challenges, learning from failures, visualizing success, and practicing gratitude, you can maintain a sense of motivation and persistence even when faced with challenges and setbacks.

Way 14

Continuously learning and improving

Continuously learning and improving is a key factor for success as an entrepreneur. Here are some important points to consider when it comes to developing your skills and improving your business:

1. Embrace a growth mindset: Embracing a growth mindset is essential for continuous learning and improvement. This means viewing challenges and setbacks as opportunities to learn and grow, and actively seeking out new knowledge and skills to improve your business.

1. Keep up with industry trends: Staying up-to-date with industry trends is important for identifying new opportunities and staying ahead of the competition. This means reading industry publications, attending conferences and networking events, and keeping tabs on what your competitors are doing.

1. Seek out feedback: Seeking out feedback from customers, employees, and other stakeholders can help you identify areas for improvement and make necessary changes to your business. This means actively soliciting feedback, both positive and negative, and being willing to make changes based on this feedback.

1. Invest in education and training: Investing in education and training can help you develop the skills and knowledge needed to succeed as an entrepreneur. This can include attending seminars and workshops, taking online courses, and pursuing advanced degrees or certifications.

1. *Surround yourself with experts: Surrounding yourself with experts in your industry or related fields can help you learn new skills and gain valuable insights into your business. This can include hiring consultants or mentors, joining industry groups or associations, or participating in networking events.*
1. *Experiment and iterate: Experimenting with new strategies and approaches can help you identify what works and what doesn't in your business. This means being willing to take calculated risks and iterate on your ideas based on what you learn along the way.*
1. *Use data to inform decision-making: Using data to inform decision-making is essential for continuous improvement. This means tracking key metrics related to your business, such as sales and customer feedback, and using this data to make informed decisions about where to focus your efforts.*
1. *Develop a culture of learning: Developing a culture of learning within your business can help encourage continuous improvement at all levels. This means setting an example as a business owner by actively seeking out new knowledge and skills, and encouraging your employees to do the same.*
1. *Stay adaptable: Staying adaptable is essential for continuous learning and improvement. This means being willing to pivot and make changes as needed based on new information or changing market conditions.*
1. *Never stop learning: Finally, the most important aspect of continuous learning and improvement is to never stop learning. This means committing to ongoing education and skill development, and continually seeking out new information and ideas to improve your business.*

In conclusion, continuous learning and improvement is essential for success as an entrepreneur. By embracing a growth mindset, keeping up with industry trends, seeking out feedback, investing in education and training, surrounding yourself with experts, experimenting and iterating, using data to inform decision-making, developing a culture of learning, staying adaptable, and never stopping learning, you can continuously improve your skills and grow your business.

Way15
Building a strong team

Building a strong team is a key component of success as an entrepreneur. Here are some important points to consider when it comes to building a strong team:

1. *Define your vision and values: The first step in building a strong team is to define your vision and values. This means articulating what you want to achieve as a business, and the values that will guide your decision-making and behaviour. With a clear vision and values, you can attract and retain team members who share your goals and beliefs.*

1. *Hire for culture fit: When hiring new team members, it's important to prioritize culture fit. This means seeking out candidates who share your values and can work effectively within your team. Look for people who are collaborative, communicative, and committed to your shared goals.*

1. *Look for diverse perspectives: While it's important to prioritize culture fit, it's also important to seek out diverse perspectives. This means looking for team members who have different backgrounds, experiences, and ways of thinking. A diverse team can bring new ideas and approaches to the table, and can*

help you better serve a wider range of customers.

1. *Set clear expectations:* Setting clear expectations is essential for building a strong team. This means articulating roles and responsibilities, as well as performance metrics and goals. By setting clear expectations, you can ensure that everyone on your team knows what is expected of them and can work together effectively.

1. *Communicate openly and frequently:* Open and frequent communication is essential for building a strong team. This means encouraging team members to share their thoughts and opinions, and providing regular feedback and updates. By fostering open communication, you can build trust and collaboration within your team.

1. *Invest in training and development:* Investing in training and development can help your team members build the skills and knowledge needed to succeed in their roles. This can include offering mentorship, providing access to training and resources, and creating opportunities for team members to learn from each other.

1. *Reward and recognize success:* Recognizing and rewarding team members for their successes can help build morale and motivation. This means offering public recognition, bonuses or other incentives, and opportunities for career advancement.

1. *Foster a positive work environment:* Fostering a positive work environment can help build a strong team. This means creating a culture of respect, kindness, and inclusivity, and providing a safe and supportive workplace. By prioritizing team members' wellbeing, you can

create a positive and productive team environment.

1. *Lead by example:* As the entrepreneur, you are the leader of your team. It's important to lead by example, setting a positive tone and embodying the values and behaviours you want to see in your team. This means being open to feedback, modelling effective communication, and taking responsibility for mistakes.

1. *Continually evaluate and improve:* Finally, building a strong team is an ongoing process. It's important to continually evaluate your team's performance, and make necessary changes to improve team dynamics and effectiveness. This means seeking out feedback, conducting regular performance reviews, and making changes as needed to help your team achieve success.

In conclusion, building a strong team is essential for success as an entrepreneur. By defining your vision and values, hiring for culture fit, looking for diverse perspectives, setting clear expectations, communicating openly and frequently, investing in training and development, rewarding and recognizing success, fostering a positive work environment, leading by example, and continually evaluating and improving, you can build a strong and effective team that will help your business achieve its goals.

Way 16
Prioritizing customer satisfaction

Prioritizing customer satisfaction is a crucial aspect of running a successful business. Here are some key points to consider when it comes to making customer satisfaction a priority:

1. *Understand your customers: The first step in prioritizing customer satisfaction is to understand your customers. This means identifying their needs and preferences, and understanding their pain points and challenges. By understanding your customers, you can tailor your products and services to meet their needs and provide a better customer experience.*
1. *Focus on service: Providing excellent customer service is essential for prioritizing customer satisfaction. This means being responsive, friendly, and helpful in all customer interactions. It also means going above and beyond to ensure that customers are satisfied with their experience.*
1. *Listen to feedback: Listening to customer feedback is an important part of prioritizing customer satisfaction. This means soliciting feedback from customers, whether through surveys, reviews, or other channels, and using that feedback to make improvements to your products and services. By actively listening to your customers, you can better understand their needs and provide a better experience.*
1. *Personalize the experience: Personalizing the customer experience is another way to prioritize customer satisfaction. This means tailoring your products and services to each individual customer's needs and preferences, and providing a personalized experience throughout the customer journey. This can include personalized product recommendations, customized marketing messages, and tailored customer support.*
1. *Resolve issues quickly: When issues arise, it's important to resolve them quickly and efficiently. This means taking ownership of problems and working to find solutions that*

meet the customer's needs. By resolving issues quickly, you can build trust with your customers and demonstrate your commitment to their satisfaction.

1. *Empower your team:* Empowering your team to prioritize customer satisfaction is essential. This means providing training and resources to help them better understand customer needs and preferences, and giving them the autonomy to make decisions that benefit the customer. By empowering your team, you can create a culture of customer service excellence that drives customer satisfaction.

1. *Use data to make informed decisions:* Data can be a powerful tool for prioritizing customer satisfaction. By tracking customer feedback, engagement, and other metrics, you can identify trends and areas for improvement, and make data-driven decisions to improve the customer experience. This can include making changes to your products and services, or adjusting your customer service approach.

1. *Continuously improve:* Prioritizing customer satisfaction is an ongoing process. It's important to continually evaluate your approach, and make improvements as needed. This means soliciting feedback, tracking metrics, and making changes to your approach based on what you learn. By continually improving, you can ensure that your customers are consistently satisfied with their experience.

In conclusion, prioritizing customer satisfaction is essential for running a successful business. By understanding your customers, focusing on service, listening to feedback, personalizing the experience, resolving issues quickly, empowering your team, using data to make informed decisions, and continuously improving, you can create a *culture of customer service excellence that drives customer satisfaction and helps your business achieve its goals.*

Way 17
Adapting to change and challenges

Adapting to change and challenges is an essential aspect of entrepreneurship. Here are some key points to consider when it comes to adapting to change and challenges:

1. *Embrace change: Change is inevitable, and successful entrepreneurs know how to embrace it. This means being open to new ideas and approaches, and being willing to take risks and try new things. By embracing change, you can stay ahead of the curve and adapt to new challenges as they arise.*
1. *Stay agile: Agility is key when it comes to adapting to change and challenges. This means being able to pivot quickly in response to new information or changing circumstances. It also means being flexible and adaptable in your approach, and being able to adjust your strategy as needed.*
1. *Be proactive: Successful entrepreneurs don't wait for change to happen – they anticipate it and take proactive steps to adapt. This means keeping an eye on industry trends and staying up-to-date on the latest developments in your field. By being proactive, you can stay ahead of the curve and be better prepared for changes and challenges that may arise.*
1. *Foster a culture of innovation: A culture of innovation can help you adapt to change and challenges more effectively. This means encouraging creativity and experimentation among your team, and fostering an*

environment where new ideas are welcomed and encouraged. By embracing innovation, you can stay ahead of the curve and adapt more quickly to new challenges.

1. Seek out new opportunities: Adapting to change and challenges also means seeking out new opportunities. This means being open to new markets and business models, and being willing to pivot your strategy in response to new opportunities that arise. By seeking out new opportunities, you can stay ahead of the curve and adapt more effectively to new challenges.

1. Be resilient: Resilience is key when it comes to adapting to change and challenges. This means being able to bounce back from setbacks and stay focused on your goals even in the face of adversity. It also means being able to learn from your failures and use them as opportunities for growth and improvement.

1. Build a strong network: Building a strong network of mentors, advisors, and peers can also help you adapt to change and challenges. This means surrounding yourself with people who can offer guidance, support, and advice as you navigate new challenges and opportunities. By building a strong network, you can tap into a wealth of knowledge and expertise to help you adapt more effectively to change.

1. Use data to inform decision-making: Data can be a powerful tool when it comes to adapting to change and challenges. By tracking metrics and analyzing data, you can identify trends and patterns that can help you make more informed decisions. This can include tracking customer feedback, monitoring industry trends, and analyzing financial data to identify opportunities for growth and improvement.

In conclusion, adapting to change and challenges is essential for entrepreneurship success. By embracing change, staying agile, being proactive, fostering a culture of innovation, seeking out new opportunities, being resilient, building a strong network, and using data to inform decision-making, you can stay ahead of the curve and adapt more effectively to new challenges and opportunities as they arise. With the right mindset and approach, you can turn even the most difficult challenges into opportunities for growth and success.

Way 18
Managing finances effectively

Managing finances effectively is an essential aspect of entrepreneurship. Here are some key points to consider when it comes to managing finances effectively:

1. *Create a budget: A budget is a crucial tool for managing finances effectively. It allows you to track your income and expenses and plan for the future. By creating a budget, you can identify areas where you may be overspending and make adjustments to stay on track.*

1. *Monitor cash flow: Monitoring cash flow is essential for managing finances effectively. It involves keeping track of the money coming in and going out of your business, and making sure you have enough cash on hand to meet your expenses. By monitoring cash flow, you can identify potential cash flow issues before they become a problem.*

1. *Minimize debt: Minimizing debt is important for managing finances effectively. This means avoiding taking on too much debt and paying off any existing debts as quickly as possible. By minimizing debt, you can reduce your*

financial risk and have more resources available to invest in your business.

1. *Keep accurate records: Keeping accurate records is essential for managing finances effectively. This means tracking all income and expenses and keeping detailed records of your financial transactions. By keeping accurate records, you can ensure you have a clear picture of your financial situation and make informed decisions about your business.*
1. *Plan for taxes: Planning for taxes is an important aspect of managing finances effectively. This means setting aside money for taxes and making sure you are in compliance with all tax laws and regulations. By planning for taxes, you can avoid any unexpected tax bills and ensure you are operating your business legally.*
1. *Invest wisely: Investing wisely is an important part of managing finances effectively. This means making smart investments that will help your business grow and thrive. It also means being cautious and avoiding high-risk investments that could jeopardize your financial stability.*
1. *Seek professional advice: Seeking professional advice is a wise move when it comes to managing finances effectively. This means working with a financial advisor or accountant who can help you create a sound financial plan and provide guidance on managing your finances. By seeking professional advice, you can benefit from their expertise and avoid common financial pitfalls.*
1. *Stay informed: Staying informed is key to managing finances effectively. This means staying up-to-date on the latest financial trends and developments, and keeping an eye on your competition. By staying informed, you can*

make informed decisions about your business and adapt to changes in the market as they arise.

In conclusion, managing finances effectively is essential for entrepreneurship success. By creating a budget, monitoring cash flow, minimizing debt, keeping accurate records, planning for taxes, investing wisely, seeking professional advice, and staying informed, you can ensure your business is on solid financial footing and set yourself up for long-term success. With a sound financial plan in place, you can focus on growing your business and achieving your goals with confidence.

Way 19
Creating a positive company culture

Creating a positive company culture is important for any business, as it can lead to improved employee morale, productivity, and customer satisfaction. Here are some key points to consider when it comes to creating a positive company culture:

1. Define your company values: Defining your company values is a critical first step in creating a positive company culture. Your values should reflect what is important to your business and guide your decision-making process.
1. Hire the right people: Hiring the right people is essential for creating a positive company culture. Look for individuals who share your company values and are committed to your business goals. Consider personality, work ethic, and communication skills when selecting new hires.
1. Foster open communication: Open communication is key to creating a positive

company culture. Encourage employees to share their ideas and opinions and be receptive to feedback. This can help to create a sense of trust and collaboration within the workplace.

1. Encourage employee development: Encouraging employee development is an important part of creating a positive company culture. Provide opportunities for training and development, and encourage employees to take on new challenges. This can help to build a culture of learning and growth within the workplace.

1. Recognize and reward employee contributions: Recognizing and rewarding employee contributions is a crucial aspect of creating a positive company culture. Acknowledge and celebrate employee successes, and consider implementing an employee recognition program. This can help to build a sense of appreciation and motivation within the workplace.

1. Foster a sense of community: Fostering a sense of community is important for creating a positive company culture. Host team-building events, encourage social interaction, and create opportunities for employees to get involved in community initiatives. This can help to build a sense of belonging and teamwork within the workplace.

1. Provide a positive work environment: Providing a positive work environment is essential for creating a positive company culture. Ensure that the workplace is clean, well-maintained, and conducive to productivity. Consider offering amenities such as healthy snacks, comfortable seating, and ergonomic workstations.

1. *Lead by example: Leading by example is crucial for creating a positive company culture. As a business owner or manager, it is important to embody the values and behaviours that you expect from your employees. By modelling positive behaviour, you can help to build a culture of respect, integrity, and accountability within the workplace.*

In conclusion, creating a positive company culture is critical for entrepreneurship success. By defining your company values, hiring the right people, fostering open communication, encouraging employee development, recognizing and rewarding employee contributions, fostering a sense of community, providing a positive work environment, and leading by example, you can create a workplace that is conducive to success. With a positive company culture in place, you can attract and retain top talent, build strong relationships with your customers, and achieve your business goals with confidence.

Way 20
Developing a marketing strategy

Developing a marketing strategy is an essential aspect of entrepreneurship. A well-crafted marketing strategy can help you to reach your target audience, build brand awareness, and drive sales. Here are some key points to consider when developing a marketing strategy:

1. *Define your target audience: Defining your target audience is the first step in developing a marketing strategy. Your target audience should be a specific group of people who are most likely to be interested in your product or service. Consider factors such as age, gender,*

location, interests, and purchasing habits when defining your target audience.

1. Research your competition: Researching your competition can help you to identify gaps in the market and refine your marketing strategy. Analyze your competitors' marketing tactics, product offerings, and pricing strategies to gain insights into what works and what doesn't.

1. Set marketing goals: Setting marketing goals is essential for developing a focused and effective marketing strategy. Consider what you want to achieve with your marketing efforts, such as increasing website traffic, generating leads, or boosting sales. Set specific, measurable goals and track your progress regularly.

1. Develop a brand identity: Developing a strong brand identity is important for building brand awareness and recognition. Consider your brand's values, personality, and visual identity, and develop a consistent brand message across all marketing channels.

1. Choose the right marketing channels: Choosing the right marketing channels is critical for reaching your target audience effectively. Consider which channels your target audience is most likely to use, such as social media, email, or print advertising. Develop a comprehensive marketing plan that includes a mix of both traditional and digital marketing channels.

1. Develop a content marketing strategy: Developing a content marketing strategy can help you to build your brand's authority and engage with your target audience. Create valuable, informative content such as blog posts, videos, and social media updates, and distribute it across your marketing channels.

1. *Measure and analyze your results: Measuring and analyzing your marketing results is essential for refining your marketing strategy and achieving your goals. Use analytics tools to track your website traffic, social media engagement, and other key metrics, and adjust your strategy based on what works best.*
1. *Develop a budget: Developing a marketing budget is essential for allocating your resources effectively and achieving your marketing goals. Consider your overall business budget and allocate a portion of it to marketing efforts. Set specific budgets for each marketing channel and track your spending to ensure that you are getting a good return on investment.*

In conclusion, developing a marketing strategy is essential for entrepreneurship success. By defining your target audience, researching your competition, setting marketing goals, developing a brand identity, choosing the right marketing channels, developing a content marketing strategy, measuring and analyzing your results, and developing a budget, you can create a marketing plan that effectively reaches your target audience and drives sales. With a strong marketing strategy in place, you can build brand awareness, establish yourself as a leader in your industry, and achieve your business goals with confidence.

Way 21
Monitoring industry trends

Monitoring industry trends is an essential aspect of entrepreneurship. Staying up to date with the latest trends and changes in your industry can help you to identify opportunities, make informed business decisions, and stay ahead of the competition. Here are some key points to consider when monitoring industry trends:

1. *Identify relevant industry sources: To stay up to date with industry trends, you need to identify relevant sources of information. Consider industry publications, blogs, trade associations, and conferences, as well as social media platforms and other online resources. Regularly review these sources to stay informed about the latest news and trends in your industry.*
1. *Analyze industry data: Analyzing industry data can provide valuable insights into the state of the industry and help you to make informed business decisions. Consider factors such as market size, growth rates, and consumer trends. Use this data to identify opportunities and make informed decisions about your business strategy.*
1. *Monitor changes in technology: Technology is constantly evolving, and staying up to date with the latest technological trends can help you to stay ahead of the competition. Monitor new technologies, tools, and platforms that are relevant to your business and consider how you can leverage them to improve your operations and better serve your customers.*
1. *Track competitor activity: Monitoring your competitors can help you to identify opportunities and refine your business strategy. Analyze your competitors' marketing efforts, product offerings, and pricing strategies, and consider how you can differentiate your business to stand out from the competition.*
1. *Keep an eye on regulatory changes: Regulatory changes can have a significant impact on your business. Stay up to date with changes to laws and regulations that are relevant to your industry, and adjust your business strategy accordingly.*

1. *Attend industry events: Attending industry events such as trade shows, conferences, and networking events can provide valuable opportunities to connect with industry leaders and stay up to date with the latest trends and developments. Use these events to network, learn from industry experts, and showcase your business.*
1. *Incorporate trends into your business strategy: Once you have identified relevant industry trends, consider how you can incorporate them into your business strategy. Identify opportunities to innovate and differentiate your business, and consider how you can leverage emerging trends to improve your operations and better serve your customers.*

In conclusion, monitoring industry trends is an essential aspect of entrepreneurship. By identifying relevant industry sources, analyzing industry data, monitoring changes in technology, tracking competitor activity, keeping an eye on regulatory changes, attending industry events, and incorporating trends into your business strategy, you can stay up to date with the latest trends and changes in your industry, make informed business decisions, and stay ahead of the competition. With a clear understanding of industry trends and a focused business strategy, you can position your business for long-term success and achieve your entrepreneurial goals with confidence.

Way 22
Embracing innovation

Embracing innovation is a key factor in the success of any business, and it is especially important for entrepreneurs who are looking to disrupt the status quo and create new products, services, and business models. Here are some key points to consider when it comes to embracing innovation in entrepreneurship:

45

1. *Foster a culture of innovation: Creating a culture that encourages and rewards innovation is critical to the success of any entrepreneurial venture. This means promoting creative thinking, encouraging risk-taking, and creating a safe space for experimentation and failure. This can be achieved by creating an open and collaborative work environment, providing resources and support for innovation, and recognising and rewarding innovative ideas and initiatives.*
1. *Identify opportunities for innovation: Innovation can take many forms, from new products and services to new business models and processes. To identify opportunities for innovation, consider what challenges and pain points exist in your industry or target market. Look for unmet needs or unsatisfied demand, and think creatively about how you can address these challenges in new and innovative ways.*
1. *Embrace emerging technologies: Emerging technologies can provide opportunities for innovation across a wide range of industries. Keep an eye on new technologies, such as artificial intelligence, blockchain, and virtual reality, and consider how they could be applied to your business. Adopting new technologies can help you to stay ahead of the competition and improve your operations, as well as create new products and services.*
1. *Collaborate with others: Collaboration can be a powerful tool for innovation. Consider partnering with other businesses, academic institutions, or industry experts to share knowledge and resources and to develop new ideas and solutions. Collaborating with others can also help to expand your network and*

open up new opportunities for growth and innovation.

1. Stay adaptable: Innovation requires flexibility and the ability to adapt to change. This means being open to new ideas and approaches, and being willing to pivot your business strategy when necessary. It also means being able to quickly respond to changes in the market, industry, or customer needs and preferences.

1. Build a diverse team: A diverse team can bring a wide range of perspectives, experiences, and skills to your business, which can help to fuel innovation. When building your team, consider diversity in terms of gender, race, ethnicity, age, and background, as well as diversity of thought and experience.

1. Test and iterate: Innovation is an iterative process, and it often requires trial and error. Test your ideas and solutions with customers and other stakeholders, and use their feedback to refine and improve your products, services, or business model. This process of testing and iteration can help you to identify and address potential problems and to refine your approach over time.

In conclusion, embracing innovation is a crucial factor in the success of any entrepreneurial venture. By fostering a culture of innovation, identifying opportunities for innovation, embracing emerging technologies, collaborating with others, staying adaptable, building a diverse team, and testing and iterating, entrepreneurs can stay ahead of the competition and create new products, services, and business models that meet the needs and preferences of their customers. With a focus on innovation and a commitment to creativity and adaptability, entrepreneurs can drive growth, create value, and achieve their entrepreneurial goals with confidence.

Way 23

Seeking out mentorship and guidance

Starting and running a successful business can be challenging, and entrepreneurs may encounter various obstacles and difficulties along the way. However, seeking out mentorship and guidance can help to overcome these challenges, and increase the chances of success. In this article, we will discuss the importance of mentorship and guidance for entrepreneurs, and how to find and work with a mentor.

Importance of Mentorship and Guidance

Mentorship and guidance can provide several benefits for entrepreneurs. These benefits include:

1. Learning from the experience of others: Mentors can offer valuable insights and guidance based on their own experiences as entrepreneurs. They can share their successes and failures, and help entrepreneurs to avoid common mistakes.
1. Expanding professional networks: Mentors can introduce entrepreneurs to potential business partners, investors, and customers. They can also provide referrals and recommendations for other resources, such as legal or accounting services.
1. Boosting confidence and motivation: Starting and running a business can be lonely and challenging, and entrepreneurs may experience self-doubt and discouragement. Mentors can provide encouragement and support, and help entrepreneurs to maintain their focus and motivation.
1. Improving decision-making skills: Mentors can help entrepreneurs to make better decisions by providing objective feedback and advice. They

can also challenge entrepreneurs to think critically and consider alternative perspectives.

Finding a Mentor

Finding a mentor can be challenging, but there are several resources and strategies that entrepreneurs can use to identify potential mentors:

1. Professional networks: Entrepreneurs can attend industry events, conferences, and workshops to meet other professionals and potential mentors. They can also join industry-specific groups and associations to expand their networks.

1. Online platforms: Online platforms, such as LinkedIn and industry-specific forums, can be useful for connecting with potential mentors. Entrepreneurs can search for professionals in their industry and send a message introducing themselves and requesting a meeting or call.

1. Referrals: Referrals from colleagues, friends, or family members can also be helpful in identifying potential mentors. Entrepreneurs can ask their network for recommendations or introductions to professionals with relevant experience and expertise.

Working with a Mentor

Once entrepreneurs have identified a potential mentor, it is important to establish a productive working relationship. Here are some tips for working with a mentor:

1. Clarify expectations: Entrepreneurs should communicate their goals and expectations to their mentor, and ask about their mentor's availability and preferred method of communication. They should also establish a schedule for regular meetings or check-ins.

1. Be open to feedback: Mentors can offer constructive feedback and criticism to help entrepreneurs improve their skills and strategies. Entrepreneurs should be open to

this feedback and take it as an opportunity to learn and grow.

1. Follow through on commitments: Entrepreneurs should be respectful of their mentor's time and expertise by following through on commitments and completing any tasks or assignments that are agreed upon.
1. Express gratitude: Entrepreneurs should express gratitude and appreciation for their mentor's guidance and support. They can do this by thanking their mentor after each meeting or check-in, and by recognizing their mentor's contributions to their success.

In Conclusion,Mentorship and guidance are essential for entrepreneurs who want to start and grow successful businesses. Mentors can provide valuable insights and guidance, expand professional networks, boost confidence and motivation, and improve decision-making skills. Entrepreneurs can find potential mentors through professional networks, online platforms, and referrals. Once a mentor is identified, it is important to establish a productive working relationship by clarifying expectations, being open to feedback, following through on commitments, and expressing gratitude. With the help of a mentor, entrepreneurs can overcome challenges, avoid common mistakes, and increase their chances of success.

Way 24
Investing in personal and professional growth

Entrepreneurship is often touted as a path to success, both personally and professionally. In order to achieve success in this field, it is important to invest in personal and professional growth. This includes developing skills, knowledge, and experience, as well as cultivating the right mindset and attitude.

One key aspect of personal growth is self-awareness. Entrepreneurs must be able to understand their own strengths and weaknesses, and be able to identify areas for improvement. This can be achieved through self-reflection, feedback from others, and ongoing learning and development.

Another important aspect of personal growth is resilience. Entrepreneurship can be a challenging and unpredictable journey, and it is important to be able to bounce back from setbacks and failures. This requires a growth mindset, which is the belief that one's abilities and intelligence can be developed through hard work and dedication.

In addition to personal growth, it is also important to invest in professional growth. This includes developing specific skills and knowledge that are relevant to the entrepreneur's field. For example, a tech entrepreneur may need to develop programming skills, while a fashion entrepreneur may need to develop design skills.

Professional growth also involves building a network of contacts and mentors who can provide support and guidance. This can be achieved through attending industry events, joining professional associations, and seeking out mentors who have experience and knowledge in the entrepreneur's field.

Another important aspect of professional growth is staying up-to-date with industry trends and developments. This requires ongoing learning and development, as well as a willingness to adapt to new technologies and changes in the marketplace.

One key strategy for investing in personal and professional growth is to seek out feedback and constructive criticism. This can be challenging, as it requires a willingness to acknowledge one's own limitations and shortcomings. However, feedback can be a valuable tool for identifying areas for improvement and developing a plan for growth.

Another strategy is to seek out opportunities for learning and development. This may involve attending conferences, taking courses, or seeking out mentorship opportunities. It is also important to stay current with industry trends and developments, and to be open to new ideas and approaches.

In addition to investing in personal and professional growth, it is important for entrepreneurs to cultivate a mindset of innovation and creativity. This involves being open to new ideas and approaches, and being willing to take risks and experiment with new concepts.

Entrepreneurship also requires a strong work ethic and a commitment to hard work and dedication. This includes being willing to put in long hours, take on challenging tasks, and persevere through setbacks and failures.

Finally, it is important for entrepreneurs to build a strong support system, both personally and professionally. This includes surrounding oneself with positive and supportive people, as well as seeking out mentors and advisors who can provide guidance and support.

In conclusion, entrepreneurship can be a path to success, both personally and professionally. However, achieving success in this field requires a commitment to personal and professional growth, as well as a mindset of innovation and creativity. By investing in oneself and staying up-to-date with industry trends and developments, entrepreneurs can position themselves for success in a rapidly changing and competitive marketplace.

Way 25
Establishing clear goals and objectives

Entrepreneurship offers individuals the opportunity to take control of their future and create their own success. One of the most important factors in achieving success as an entrepreneur is establishing clear goals and objectives for your business.

Having clear goals and objectives is essential for guiding decision-making and measuring progress. It allows entrepreneurs to focus their efforts on the activities that will have the greatest impact on their business.

When setting goals and objectives, it is important to ensure they are specific, measurable, attainable, relevant, and time-bound. This means defining what you want to achieve, how you will measure success, ensuring that the goals are realistic and relevant to your business, and setting a deadline for achieving them.

One way to establish clear goals and objectives is by conducting a SWOT analysis. This involves identifying your business's strengths, weaknesses, opportunities, and threats. By doing so, you can identify areas where you need to improve and opportunities that you can capitalize on. This can help you set goals and objectives that are relevant and achievable.

Another important consideration when setting goals and objectives is to align them with your vision and mission. This means ensuring that the goals and objectives you set are consistent with the long-term aspirations of your business. By doing so, you can ensure that you are building a business that is aligned with your personal and professional aspirations.

Once you have established clear goals and objectives, it is important to track progress and adjust course as needed. This means regularly monitoring performance and making adjustments to your strategy as necessary. By doing so, you can ensure that you are on track to achieving your goals and can make any necessary changes to stay on course.

It is also important to communicate your goals and objectives to your team. This can help ensure that everyone is working towards the same goals and can help align efforts towards achieving them. It can also help create a sense of accountability and can encourage team members to take ownership of their work.

In addition to setting clear goals and objectives, there are other key factors that can contribute to entrepreneurial success. These include having a clear vision for your business, developing a solid business plan, and having a strong support system in place.

Having a clear vision for your business means understanding your target market, identifying your unique value proposition, and setting clear goals and objectives. This can help guide decision-making and ensure that you are building a business that is aligned with your personal and professional aspirations.

Developing a solid business plan means outlining your marketing strategy, financial projections, and operational processes. By doing so, you can identify potential challenges and opportunities and develop a plan for addressing them.

Finally, having a strong support system in place can be essential for entrepreneurial success. This may include family and friends who can offer encouragement and support, as well as mentors or coaches who can provide guidance and advice.

In conclusion, establishing clear goals and objectives is a critical factor in achieving success as an entrepreneur. By setting specific, measurable, attainable, relevant, and time-bound goals, entrepreneurs can focus their efforts on the activities that will have the greatest impact on their business. It is also important to align these goals with your vision and mission, track progress, and adjust course as needed. By doing so, entrepreneurs can build a business that is aligned with their personal and professional aspirations and increase their chances of long-term success.

Way 26
Balancing work and personal life

Starting a business can be a time-consuming and all-encompassing task, but it is important for entrepreneurs to prioritize balancing their work and personal lives in order to achieve long-term success.

One of the first steps in balancing work and personal life is to set boundaries. This means setting specific work hours *and sticking to them, as well as making time for personal activities and relationships. It is also important to prioritize self-care, including exercise, healthy eating, and adequate rest.*

Another key factor in balancing work and personal life is delegation. Entrepreneurs may feel that they need to do everything themselves, but it is important to delegate tasks to employees or contractors where possible. This not only frees up time for personal activities, but can also help to build a strong team and promote business growth.

Technology can also be a helpful tool for balancing work and personal life. Using tools such as scheduling software, email filters, and messaging apps can help to streamline communication and reduce the time required for administrative tasks. However, it is important to set boundaries around technology use to prevent it from becoming a source of stress or distraction.

In addition to setting boundaries and delegating tasks, it is important for entrepreneurs to establish a support network. This may include family and friends who can provide emotional support and encouragement, as well as mentors or business advisors who can offer guidance and expertise. It may also be helpful to join networking groups or attend industry events to connect with other entrepreneurs and gain new perspectives.

Entrepreneurs should also prioritize self-reflection and personal growth. This may include setting personal goals and working towards them, as well as seeking feedback and constructive criticism from others. Investing in personal growth can not only help to prevent burnout, but can also enhance business success by improving leadership skills and fostering innovation.

Finally, it is important for entrepreneurs to be flexible and adaptable in their approach to work and personal life. Life is unpredictable, and unexpected challenges or opportunities may arise. By remaining open to change and being willing to adjust their priorities as needed, entrepreneurs can maintain a healthy balance between work and personal life and achieve long-term success.

In summary, balancing work and personal life is essential for entrepreneurial success. Setting boundaries, delegating tasks, using technology wisely, establishing a support network, investing in personal growth, and remaining flexible and adaptable are all important factors in achieving a healthy balance. By prioritizing self-care and personal relationships, entrepreneurs can avoid burnout and maintain a positive outlook, while also building a successful business that is aligned with their personal and professional aspirations.

Way 27
Creating a strong personal brand

Entrepreneurship is all about creating something from scratch, which often includes building a personal brand. A personal brand is the reputation and image that an individual portrays to others. It can be seen as a crucial component in the success of any entrepreneur, as it distinguishes them from the competition and establishes them as an expert in their field. Here are some tips for creating a strong personal brand.

1. Define Your Brand Identity

Before building a personal brand, you must first define your brand identity. This means understanding what you want to be known for, what your strengths are, and what makes you unique. You must also have a clear understanding of your target audience and what they need or want from you. By identifying your unique selling points, you can create a strong personal brand that resonates with your audience.

1. Create a Consistent Brand Image

Consistency is key when it comes to building a strong personal brand. This means that all aspects of your brand, including your website, social media profiles, and marketing materials, should have a consistent look and feel. This helps to establish credibility and trust with your audience, which can ultimately lead to increased business opportunities.

1. Establish Your Expertise

As an entrepreneur, it's essential to establish yourself as an expert in your field. This means sharing your knowledge and insights through blog posts, social media updates, and other forms of content. By demonstrating your expertise, you can build trust with your audience and establish yourself as a thought leader in your industry.

1. Network and Build Relationships

Networking is an essential part of building a successful personal brand. Attend industry events, connect with other professionals in your field, and look for opportunities to collaborate with others. Building relationships with other entrepreneurs and industry experts can help to expand your reach and increase your visibility.

1. Use Social Media Effectively

Social media is a powerful tool for building a personal brand. It provides a platform for you to showcase your expertise, connect with others in your industry, and reach a wider audience. To use social media effectively, it's important to create a consistent brand image across all platforms and to engage with your audience regularly.

1. Be Authentic

Authenticity is a key component of a strong personal brand. Your brand should reflect who you are as a person and what you stand for. Don't try to be someone you're not, as this can come across as disingenuous and ultimately harm your reputation.

1. Monitor Your Reputation

Once you've established a personal brand, it's important to monitor your reputation. This means regularly checking online reviews, social media comments, and other forms of feedback. By monitoring your reputation, you can address any negative feedback or complaints quickly and maintain a positive image.

In conclusion, building a strong personal brand is an essential component of success as an entrepreneur. By defining your brand identity, creating a consistent brand image, establishing your expertise, networking and building relationships, using social media effectively, being authentic, and monitoring your reputation, you can create a personal brand that resonates with your audience and helps you stand out in a crowded marketplace.

Way 28
Collaborating with others

Collaboration is a crucial part of entrepreneurship, as it enables entrepreneurs to access resources and expertise that they may not have on their own. Collaborating with others can also help entrepreneurs to expand their network, increase their visibility, and access new business opportunities. Here are some tips for collaborating effectively as an entrepreneur.

1. Identify Potential Collaborators

The first step in collaborating effectively is to identify potential collaborators. This means seeking out individuals or organizations that share your vision, values, and goals. Look for individuals or organizations that complement your skills and expertise and can provide value to your business.

1. Establish Clear Goals and Expectations

Before entering into a collaboration, it's essential to establish clear goals and expectations. This means defining what each party hopes to achieve from the collaboration and establishing timelines, deliverables, and other key performance indicators. By setting clear goals and expectations, you can ensure that everyone is on the same page and working towards a common goal.

1. Communication is Key

Effective communication is critical in any collaboration. This means establishing regular check-ins, sharing updates on progress, and being transparent about any challenges or roadblocks. By communicating effectively, you can build trust with your collaborators and ensure that everyone is working towards a shared vision.

1. Focus on Mutual Benefit

Collaboration should be mutually beneficial for all parties involved. This means identifying how each party can contribute to the collaboration and what they stand to gain from it. By focusing on mutual benefit, you can ensure that everyone is motivated and committed to the collaboration.

1. Be Open to New Ideas

Collaborating with others can bring new ideas and perspectives to the table. As an entrepreneur, it's essential to be open to new ideas and receptive to feedback from your collaborators. By being open-minded, you can create a collaborative environment that fosters creativity and innovation.

1. Establish Trust

Trust is essential in any collaboration. This means being reliable, following through on commitments, and being transparent about any challenges or roadblocks. By establishing trust with your collaborators, you can create a collaborative environment that is supportive and productive.

1. Have a Clear Process for Decision Making

In any collaboration, it's essential to have a clear process for decision making. This means establishing who has the final say on important decisions and how decisions will be made. By having a clear process for decision making, you can avoid conflicts and ensure that everyone is working towards a common goal.

1. Recognize and Celebrate Success

Collaboration can be hard work, but it can also be incredibly rewarding. As you work with your collaborators, be sure to recognize and celebrate your successes. This means acknowledging the contributions of all parties involved and taking the time to reflect on what you've achieved together. In conclusion, collaborating with others is an essential part of entrepreneurship. By identifying potential collaborators, establishing clear goals and expectations, communicating effectively, focusing on mutual benefit, being open to new ideas, establishing trust, having a clear process for decision making, and recognizing and celebrating success, you can collaborate effectively and achieve your business goals. Collaboration requires a willingness to be flexible, listen to feedback, and work together towards a shared vision. As an entrepreneur, collaboration can be the key to unlocking new opportunities, building your network, and achieving success.

Way 29
Embracing failure as a learning opportunity

Failure is an inevitable part of entrepreneurship. However, instead of seeing failure as the end of the road, entrepreneurs should embrace it as a learning opportunity. Embracing failure means taking responsibility for your mistakes, learning from them, and using them to grow and improve. Here are some tips for embracing failure as an entrepreneur.

1. Take Responsibility for Your Mistakes

The first step in embracing failure is to take responsibility for your mistakes. This means acknowledging what went wrong, accepting the consequences of your actions, and owning up to your part in the failure. By taking responsibility for your mistakes, you can learn from them and avoid making the same mistakes in the future.

1. Learn from Your Mistakes

Once you've taken responsibility for your mistakes, the next step is to learn from them. This means reflecting on what went wrong, identifying the factors that contributed to the failure, and figuring out what you could have done differently. By learning from your mistakes, you can avoid repeating them in the future and improve your chances of success.

1. Don't Be Afraid to Experiment

As an entrepreneur, it's essential to be willing to experiment and try new things. This means being open to taking risks and embracing the possibility of failure. By experimenting, you can learn what works and what doesn't, and refine your approach over time.

1. Persevere Through Setbacks

Failure can be demotivating, but it's important not to give up when faced with setbacks. Instead, use failures as a source of motivation and as an opportunity to learn and grow. Perseverance is a key trait of successful entrepreneurs, and by persevering through setbacks, you can build resilience and develop the skills necessary to achieve your goals.

1. *Embrace a Growth Mindset*

A growth mindset is the belief that your abilities can be developed through hard work, dedication, and a willingness to learn. By embracing a growth mindset, you can view failure as an opportunity to learn and improve, rather than a reflection of your abilities. This means being open to feedback, seeking out new challenges, and continuously learning and growing as an entrepreneur.

1. *Surround Yourself with Supportive People*

Surrounding yourself with supportive people is critical in embracing failure. This means seeking out mentors, advisors, and other entrepreneurs who can provide guidance, support, and encouragement when faced with setbacks. By surrounding yourself with supportive people, you can build a strong network and gain valuable insights and perspective.

1. *Stay Positive and Focus on the Big Picture*

Staying positive and focusing on the big picture is crucial in embracing failure. Instead of dwelling on past mistakes, focus on the lessons you've learned and the progress you've made. By staying positive and keeping your eye on the big picture, you can maintain a sense of perspective and stay motivated to achieve your goals.

In conclusion, embracing failure as a learning opportunity is essential in entrepreneurship. By taking responsibility for your mistakes, learning from them, experimenting, persevering through setbacks, embracing a growth mindset, surrounding yourself with supportive people, and staying positive and focused on the big picture, you can use failure as a source of motivation and a tool for growth. Failure can be challenging, but by reframing it as an opportunity to learn and improve, you can build the resilience, skills, and mindset necessary to achieve success in entrepreneurship.

Way 30
Giving back to the community

1. Giving back to the community is an essential aspect of entrepreneurship. Not only does it help to build a positive reputation for your business, but it also allows you to make a meaningful impact on the world around you. Here are some tips for giving back to the community as an entrepreneur.

1. Identify the Needs of Your Community

The first step in giving back to the community is to identify its needs. This means researching the issues facing your community and finding ways that your business can make a meaningful impact. By understanding the needs of your community, you can focus your efforts on areas where you can make the most significant difference.

1. Volunteer Your Time and Resources

Volunteering your time and resources is an excellent way to give back to the community. This means getting involved in local charities, non-profit organizations, and community initiatives. By volunteering your time and resources, you can help to address the needs of your community, build relationships with local stakeholders, and gain a better understanding of the challenges facing your community.

1. Donate to Local Charities and Causes

Donating to local charities and causes is another way to give back to the community. This means identifying organizations that align with your business's values and making financial contributions to support their work. By donating to local charities and causes, you can help to address the needs of your community and build a positive reputation for your business.

1. Support Local Businesses

Supporting local businesses is another way to give back to the community. This means sourcing products and services from local businesses and collaborating with them on community initiatives. By supporting local businesses, you can help to create jobs, boost the local economy, and strengthen the fabric of your community.

1. *Partner with Non-Profit Organizations*

Partnering with non-profit organizations is another way to give back to the community. This means collaborating with organizations that share your business's values and mission to address the needs of your community. By partnering with non-profit organizations, you can leverage your resources and expertise to make a meaningful impact on your community.

1. *Launch Community Initiatives*

Launching community initiatives is another way to give back to the community. This means creating programs and projects that address the needs of your community and align with your business's values and mission. By launching community initiatives, you can make a tangible impact on the world around you and build a positive reputation for your business.

1. *Build a Sustainable Business*

Building a sustainable business is another way to give back to the community. This means creating a business that has a positive impact on the environment and society. By prioritizing sustainability, you can help to reduce the environmental impact of your business, create a more equitable society, and build a more sustainable future for everyone.

In conclusion, giving back to the community is an essential aspect of entrepreneurship. By identifying the needs of your community, volunteering your time and resources, donating to local charities and causes, supporting local businesses, partnering with non-profit organizations, launching community initiatives, and building a sustainable business, you can make a meaningful impact on the world around you and build a positive reputation for your business. Giving back to the community is not only the right thing to do, but it's also good for business, and it can help to create a better world for everyone.

www.ingramcontent.com/pod-product-compliance
Lightning Source LLC
Chambersburg PA
CBHW070750220526
45467CB00018B/1735